THE PORTAGE POETRY SERIES

I0521726

Praise for
Monarch

"I'll never see dentures the same, or the California flag or a pearl brooch or river rock or shame. Heather Bourbeau chronicles the flotsam of human effort—both destructive and reparative—over the West Coast of the North American continent. She's convinced me there's no better way to get history than poetry. I feel close to these figures (both human and nonhuman) that time, greed, hypocrisy, and desperation have stolen from us. *Monarch* leaves you splashed with feeling and leavened with learning."

—Lulu Miller
author of *Why Fish Don't Exist* and Co-Host of Radiolab

"There are many histories of the western United States and they are not all created equal. In *Monarch*, poet Heather Bourbeau gives a master class in what the poet's eye can make of some of these histories. Make no mistake, this is not history as a dry and emotionless drumroll, *Monarch* is heat lightning: 'How do you bury bodies gathered in pieces by search parties with gunnysacks?' This collection reveals, unfolds, different stories each time you read it. You should read it."

—Kim Shuck
Seventh Poet Laureate of San Francisco Emerita

"There's a brutality to history, to honesty, to truth, a stripped down power that doesn't allow much room for pretense and forgiveness. But there is also a beauty that beams hope. *Monarch* by Heather Bourbeau is such a record, a history of us distilled to a raw violence that comes through the record keeping done by a poet, an artist. I couldn't feel the final page of the book because a work like this is not meant to wrap up, but to trigger beginnings of reckonings, of repentance, of a collective desire to hope for a better legacy for human kind. It's such a book of loud screams and silent introspection. Bourbeau has shared with us something of incredible power."

—Chiwan Choi
author of *my name is wolf*

"*Monarch* is a stunning poetry collection. Using her keen, unsparing eye, author Heather Bourbeau combines personal history with regional histories of California, Nevada, Oregon, and Washington. The result is a dazzling guide to the past that thrums like a beating heart. I could not stop reading these poems, lingered over every detail and description, from the timelines to the life stories of the known and the unknown; from the cost of a fried grizzly dinner in the title poem to the complicity of shopping mall goers in 'Black Friday' to the pastor's life in 'Fire Balloon' and the lists of detritus after a volcanic eruption or a large gathering such as Burning Man. This book is necessary and important, and should be taught in schools."

—Devi S. Laskar
author of *The Atlas of Reds and Blues* and *Circa*

"Like the Western United States itself, Heather Bourbeau's poems are persistently discoverable over successive explorations. Each piece in *Monarch* is meticulously structured to render one awed and haunted by its simultaneous complexity and accessibility. She mines the fragilities and inflexible elements of the Earth, nature, and human beings themselves with extraordinary grace. The women and men in works such as 'Fire Balloon (Fu-Go)' and 'El Honor de Luis' are evocative tragi-heroes desperately clutching hold to dissipating prayers, dreams deferred. Trees, wind, rock, and dirt are strikingly personified as vividly as any human character in literature, breathing life, destruction, and balance into dizzying ecosystems intentionally construed by Bourbeau to haunt long after pages are turned. *Monarch* is a collection of poetry offering historically-framed sagas filled with varying scope and heart-wrenching emotion, but with careful spareness, dry as a bone."

—Jimmie Briggs
Principal, Skoll Foundation

"*Monarch*, Heather Bourbeau's poetic pickaxe, excavates with great care and precision the forgotten, living US Western history and offers some equilibrium we'll need for sustainable struggle. Traversing and connecting with stories from the diverse regions of the Pacific Northwest, Bourbeau embodies in word and deed the spirit that will help heal the ravages of frontier history."

—Roberto Lovato
author of *Unforgetting*

MONARCH

Heather Bourbeau

Cornerstone Press
Stevens Point, Wisconsin

Cornerstone Press, Stevens Point, Wisconsin 54481
Copyright © 2023 Heather Bourbeau
www.uwsp.edu/cornerstone

Printed in the United States of America by
Point Print and Design Studio, Stevens Point, Wisconsin

Library of Congress Control Number: 2022946139
ISBN: 979-8-9861447-9-5

All rights reserved.

Cornerstone Press titles are produced in courses and internships offered by the
Department of English at the University of Wisconsin–Stevens Point.

DIRECTOR & PUBLISHER   EXECUTIVE EDITOR
Dr. Ross K. Tangedal   Jeff Snowbarger

SENIOR EDITORS
Lexie Neeley, Monica Swinick, Kala Buttke

PRESS STAFF
Alyssa Bronk, Grace Dahl, Patrick Fogarty, Angela Green, Cal Henkens, Brett Hill, Ryan Jensen,
Julia Kaufman, Hunter Kiesow, Adam King, Amanda Leibham, Maria Scherer, Abbi Wasielewski

For my father

Contents

CALIFORNIA

NEVADA

OREGON

WASHINGTON

CALIFORNIA

Salmon River Timeline[1]

850-1300 Wiyot, Yurok, Karuk, and Hupa arrive in the Klamath Basin.

1826 First journal record of British fur trapper in Siskiyou County.

1849 First discovery by whites of gold along the Salmon River. The next year, white prospectors begin arriving.

1851 Karuk villages, including the sacred villages of Yutamin and Katamin, burned by white settlers and miners in 1851 and 1852.

1852 State of California enacts the first fish and game law to protect specific species including deer, quail, waterfowl, and salmon.

1850s Scott Valley described as having "small deer; lots of big dogs [wolves], lots of small dogs [coyote]; lots of big bears with white faces; and small bears, both black and brown. The creeks and river were full of many kinds of fish, and there are beaver and many small animals."

1862 Homestead Act signed into law. Provides any adult citizen with 160 acres of surveyed government land in the West.

1866 Mineral Grant of 1866 opens public lands to hard rock prospecting and mining and allows the transfer of claims into private ownership.

Late 1860s/Early 1870s First hydraulic mine on the South Fork.

1872 General Mining Act of 1872 authorizes mining on federal public lands.

1891 Forest Reserve Act establishes forest reserves within the Department of the Interior. Will later become the National Forest System.

1900 Elk eradicated from the Klamath.

1902 Last grizzly recorded being killed in Northern California, near Hornbrook.

1905   Klamath Forest Reserve established (to later become the Klamath National Forest).

1906   Newly established Reclamation Service initiates the Klamath Project to drain lakes and wetlands for cultivation.

1910   Logging becomes a growing industry in the region.

1912   Three salmon cannery plants operate on or near the Klamath River estuary.

1921   Fish planting in the Salmon River Ranger District to replenish depleted stocks.

1924   Last wild wolf in California is trapped in Lassen County.

Post WWII-Early 1990s   Logging boom leads to clear-cutting and liquidating of old growth forests.

1964   Wilderness Act passed, designating Marble Mountain Wilderness protected.

1970   National Environmental Policy Act enacted.

1973   Endangered Species Act enacted.

1977   California's snowpack reaches an all-time low.

1984   Trinity Alps and Russian Wilderness Areas created.

1990-1994   Elk are reintroduced.

1997   Coho salmon federally listed as a threatened species.

2002   The largest salmon kill in Western US history occurs when at least 80,000 salmon are killed by disease, exacerbated or directly caused by low river flows due to US Bureau of Reclamation water diversions during a drought year.

2009   Suction dredge mining banned in California.

2011   First wild wolf enters California since 1924.

2012   Court ruling states that even recreational-scale mining is subject to the Endangered Species Act.

2013   California experiences the driest year on record, possibly the driest since 1580 based on tree rings.

2014   Early snowpack levels higher than normal. By May, however, record low snowpack reported at 0% of normal.

Dec. 2016-Mar. 2017   Wettest winter on record.

Jun. 2017-Oct. 2017   Nearly 67,000 acres burn in the Salmon River Watershed.

A Man Named Remembrance
Recalls the Gold Rush[2]

Ten years before the Civil War, men are testing the newest state
borne from greed and god and rape. They have gathered in the hills, lived

hip-deep in creeks and riverbeds, among beaver dams and willows.
Even as a child, Remembrance knows all the gold will be pulled by brute and luck

from Deer Creek. Prospectors press the last glint from rock,
suck the shine from the rich alluvium soil. July 4th the shantytowns alight

with alcohol, hurdy-gurdy girls, and the promise of a fight between a bear
and a bull, the two entwined. A frenzy of pheromones and fear,

matched by men who batter and pan 10 hours each spring and summer day,
using the rush of water melting above to dredge and discover

something worth having left everything else behind. Small dogs bloody the bear,
young men hang garlands from the bull's horns. Each passion play

has its archetype. Here is the raw beastliness of the native grizzly, there the manliness
of the Spanish steer. The Maidu and Paiute are being beaten, the Chinese forced to pay

$5 for the privilege of mining land whiter migrants claim to own. One of these,
who finds their souls refreshed by the sight of beasts of blood, will lose

his life—not from man or beast—but from his own gun as he tries and fails
to force the grizzly from its den. [I am momentarily pleased.

Karma and Darwin have each won a point. But hiding in my heart is an envy I try
to deny—of striking out, of feeling fresh earth, of being clever or lucky enough

to make a fortune that can be passed down before my peers can see the perversity
and pain, before my deeds can be written by my grateful, ignorant son.]

Monarch, the Last California Grizzly

Ursus arctos californicus
> *Bear*

Monarch
> *To rule alone*

Colin Preston killed 200 grizzlies in one season.
Mariposa hotel served fried grizzly for 75 cents.
A trapper made furniture from bear parts, presented a chair
to President Johnson. Four legs and claws, a cord to push
the head, its gnashing teeth from under the seat.

In 1889, Hearst asked a reporter to become a hunter,
capture the last wild grizzly. Five months later, deep
in southern coastal wilderness, lured by honey and mutton,
Monarch was captured.

Gagged and collared, one leg "well-anchored,"
a rope around his loins, tethered to trees at night.
He bit and tore at restraints, chewed the chains,
splintered his teeth, spattered the trap with bloody froth.

In San Francisco, Monarch was fêted and feared,
moved from gardens to park to zoo. By the Midwinter Exposition,
the ostriches drew more spectators. But in '06,
a city beaten by quake and fire looked to Monarch's survival for inspiration.

Five years later, he would be put down,
skinned and stuffed. His remains buried, then exhumed.
His skull lost, cracked, and broken. His taxidermied body—
the model for the new state flag.

On the white background, red star to left,
walks a bear, head bent slightly, mouth open, teeth bright,
free to feel the soft and rough of the ground,
the green underneath its unchained feet.

Hercules Powder Works[3]

Gunpowder birthplace gone. They worked nitro lines,
created dreams of death—smokeless and black, sharpshooter and bullseye,
thin flakes for short-barreled guns.

Eucalyptus replaced redwood and willow, madrone and alder,
plucked and pulped for dynamite.
Fast-growing blue gum a better buffer for uncontrolled explosions.

> *under the gingko, under the earth*

Nitroglycerine and mixing houses, risk and reward.
60-hours, $7.50-a-week for Chinese, $50-a-week for whites.
Blasts mistaken for earthquakes, felt as far as Oakland.

1883 explosion: 40 Chinese men and one white man dead.
1895 explosion: nine Chinese men and two white men dead.
1908 explosion: 20 Chinese men and one white man dead.

> *under the gingko, under the earth*

One mile from factory ruins, near pubs and pet stores named "Powder Keg,"
is a park where children swing on monkey bars, unaware.
Under a young gingko is one plaque to the factory's Chinese laborers.

How do you bury bodies gathered in pieces by search parties with gunnysacks?
How were these men mourned by their families back home
who never knew their fate?

Allensworth

When you reimagine landscapes and liberties, you must remember
who controls the drip and drought controls the dream.

Allen Allensworth, born a slave, became seaman, minister, Kentucky delegate
to Republican National Conventions.

1908 Owens Valley farmers were cast aside for an aqueduct to slake Los Angeles
1908 Allensworth left the City of Angels to build a new Eden—

Central Valley railroad depot, fertile soil, access to water. Founded, financed,
and governed by Blacks. Free of racism. Able to blossom and thrive.

Four years later, 100 residents welcomed Alwortha Hall, the first baby born.
Two general stores, post office, school, library. Bakery, drug store, hotel.

Poultry and sugar beet farms, plaster and carpentry shops.
Girl's Glee Club, Children's Savings Association, Debating Society.

But the Railway built a spur to avoid town, refused to hire Blacks as depot's
manager or ticket agent. Pacific Farming never delivered enough water.

And as James Meredith was shot trying to march across the Mississippi Delta,
arsenic was found in Allensworth's water. The town was scheduled for demolition

In the Golden State, all roads begin and end with water.
At town's dedication, Allensworth, the man, had said, "We must do as they did—

settle upon the bare desert, cause it to bloom like a rose." (But Adam and Eve
had Pishon, Gihon, Chidekel, and Phirat pouring forth from a single source.)

In 1908, the Tulare Basin fed artesian wells, alfalfa, corn, and livestock.
Men harvested fish with buckets. Twenty years later, Tulare Lake had been drained dry

After the Gold Rush

Riparian corridors wended to silty loam, heavy
clay soils, alkali salts. Delta dreams ebbed and flowed.
Chinese forced to leave. Japanese streamed in. Railroads, mines,
and farms. Rice imported from Asia, South America.

Where the Maidu tended oak for acorns, gathered greens and berries,
Kenju Ikuta showed the possibility of grain from hardpan soil,
black adobe. Profit and praise. Rice became the new gold.
One year later, Japanese could not own farms.

In 1920, the Committee on Immigration and Naturalization
read a pamphlet by Chester Versteeg. California, he wrote, owed
a debt to the Japanese. Called Ikuta "a pioneer." But they were not,
he argued, entitled to have land, be citizens.

In World War II, rice plantings delayed, fields foul with weeds,
Issei, *Nisei*, and *Sansei* were gathered and interned. Became field hands
for government farms. Potatoes and daikon, grains and hay
sold on open markets.

In 1964, rice production at record highs,
24 years before reparations,
the US Board on Geographic Names designated a summit
that overlooks Manzanar, 20 miles to the east, "Mount Versteeg."

When I was young, I grew near the remnants of Japantown,
was told of Manzanar and Tule Lake by neighbors, fathers of friends.
When I was young, my seasons were marked by rice.
Spring meant flooding planted wetlands. Fall—the burn after harvests.

Black Friday

Temescal Creek, small hill of tools, bowls, animal bones. Ate and traded.
Honored life from the Bay. Mussels and oysters, clams and cockles.
Remains of ancestors. Flex the body, knees under chin,
hands against cheeks. Wrapped in blankets, buried with shells.
2000 years. Lisjan. Ohlone.

Spanish came. Ignored the mound. Spanish went. Gold Rush drive. Desolation.
Desecration. In 1853, across the Bay, North Beach Cemetery removed,
graves relocated, corpses heaped onto roadside, shoveled into carts.
Shards of rotting coffins sold for firewood. At Yerba Buena Cemetery,
body parts stolen to make soap.

1876. Centennial America. Amusement park built on Emeryville Shellmound.
Race track and carousel. Bowling alley and shooting range.
Railway for easy access. Hilltop leveled for party pavilion.
Stairway to top, sheltered by cypress. Views for partygoers,
dancing on graves.

1924. Prohibition meant sale. Shellmound for Sherwin-Williams.
Lead-based paints, dry lime sulfur pesticides.
Mound leveled. Soil choked on arsenic and acid.
700 remains found, moved to Berkeley campus.
The foul and the sacred.

1999. New development, new discoveries. Intact burials. Men and women,
limbs entwined. Mothers and babies. Bodies under stone mortar.
Bones rubberized by arsenic exposure. Bones broken by backhoes.
Some shipped with toxic soil to Texas and burned.
300 bodies reburied on site of shopping mall.

Now Ohlone Way and Shellmound Street lead to movie theater and restaurants,
Victoria's Secret and H&M, apartments and townhomes. Near Old Navy, ersatz
creek and shellmound, sculpture of Ohlone basket, timeline of Ohlone history.
But no sign to say you are walking over the dead,
no way to know your complicity.

De Colores

California was not first, but best at "better breeding."
70 years. 20,000 people. Scars and scabs. *Son colores, son colores.*

Do not be horrified only by the science of Nazis,
they turned to the Golden State to learn our ways.

Fertility in a poor woman, sin. In a woman of color, threat.
1927 Supreme Court said, instead of inevitable crime or starving

or stupidity, "better for all the world" to stop the unfit from "continuing their kind."
In the name of the dollar, and of the not-so-Native sons.

15-year-old girl. Sonoma State Home. Orphaned. History of emotional instability,
feeblemindedness. "After careful consideration" by medical staff, tubes removed.

"Hyper-fertile," "criminally inclined," "delinquent." The Latina womb is perilous.
Depression-era "repatriations" not enough. *Son colores, son colores.*

18-year-old woman. "Sexually wayward." Went to hotel with man for sex.
State asked father's permission to sterilize. He refused. State persisted.

As if this were not Mexico first. 1970s, Mexican immigrant women
gave birth in LA County Hospital. Emergency C-sections. Tubes tied without

consent. A lawsuit. A state shamed. A practice banned.
But prisons have always been outside the law. Black and Latina women

would wake into menopause for the crime of being. Until the leaves
began to brown in 2014. *Son colores, son colores.*

My mother was poor but white, troubled teen mom.
My mother was in an institution. My mother could have been Iris or Andrea,

but instead, I was a newborn held in awe by my family, full of faults and love.
Instead, I am here to write their stories. *Son colores, son colores.*
De gente que sabe de la libertad.

El Honor de Luis[4]

I was an immigrant.
Classic American tale. Farmworker wanting better
for my children. 3,000 miles. 14 years. Missed
birthdays and baptisms. Remittances and remembrance.
So few spoke my language here.
                For this, should I be killed?

I was Maya.
Corn fields and altars, Quetzalcoatl and Kukulkan,
chaya and loros, jarana and guayaberas,
yucca and honey. Small home built
with money sent over seven years.
                For this?

I was a Mexican.
Sold horse and summer harvest to join my brother
North. Milagro and Virgin. Found work and community,
house of mold and bed bugs, rodents and roaches.
Five men, two beds, beer and soccer.
                For this?

April 7, 2016, in need of food and shelter,
counselor and advocate, I became a number.
Thirty seconds. Four bean bag shots. Seven bullets.
As I lay on the ground.

Even if you never knew my name,
In kuxtal, my life had value.
Flowers and candles, photos and saints.

Ask my wife who seeks answers and comfort.
Ask my mother who had to bury her child.
Ask the trees that still long for the air
I once breathed.

Items Found on Angel Island

black-tailed deer bones, sea lion whiskers, bat ray caudal spines,
bird bone tubes, bone needles, flat pins from large mammal long bone shafts,
polished bones, butchered bones,
isolated human bone fragments, presumed grave goods,

shell beads, shell ornaments, shell fishhooks,
net and fishing weights, milling slabs, mortars, pestles,
handstones, hammerstones, stone beads, pendants, charmstones,
awls, arrowheads, baked clay,

ceramic doll parts, a mother-of-pearl brooch,
buttons, belt buckles,
hardware from clocks, miniature teacups,
milk bottles, beer bottles from the 1890s, liquor bottles from World War II,

Indian Head penny stamped with "Liberty,"
military cartridge from when the island was training ground for US soldiers serving
in campaigns against the Apache, Sioux, Modoc, and other Native American tribes,

220 Chinese poems, 96 Chinese inscriptions, 89 English inscriptions,
62 Japanese inscriptions, 33 Chinese graphic images
by immigrants prevented from entering the United States.

NEVADA

Ghost Dance Timeline

1830   Indian Removal Act is signed into law.

1844   Pyramid Lake is "discovered" by John C. Fremont while on a mapping expedition for the US government.

1856   The Paiute prophet Quoitze Ow, also known as Wovoka, is born in western Nevada.

1860   The First Battle of Pyramid Lake takes place in May as Northern Paiutes defeat a volunteer army of whites from Virginia City and nearby settlements. As a result, the colonists call a former Texas Ranger to help organize and train another volunteer regiment. The US Army also sends troops from California.

1860   The Second Battle of Pyramid Lake takes place in June. The US and volunteer armies defeat the Northern Paiute. US Army soldiers build several forts around the lake.

1860s-80s Comstock Lode triggers a mass immigration of miners and pioneers.

1860   The Army forts around Pyramid Lake are abandoned and construction begins on a larger fort along the Carson River, Fort Churchill.

1865   An education statute prohibits African-Americans, Asians, Asian-Americans, and Native Americans from attending public schools in Nevada. Separate schools for the education of African-Americans, Asians, Asian-Americans, and Native Americans could be created if "advisable."

1867   A typhoid epidemic kills approximately one-tenth of the Walker River Paiutes. The following year, measles kills twenty-five Paiutes. These outbreaks take an economic and psychological toll.

1869   Wodziwob ("Gray Hair"), a Northern Paiute, has a dream that he believes empowers him to lead those that had died in previous months back to their grieving families. He organizes a series of dances and announces his powers.

1870   As a result of visionary experiences, Wodziwob initiates the early phase of the Ghost Dance at the Walker River Reservation. He was told in these visions that an Indian tribal life would soon return, the dead would come back to life, and animals the Indians hunted would come back. In order to hasten these events, Wodziwob says Indians should perform specific round dances at night. The movement soon spreads to other tribes and is practiced in California and Oregon.

1870s   The Ghost Dancers become disillusioned with the movement and the majority disband, although among other tribal nations in California, some offshoots such as Earth Lodge and Big Head ceremonies continue to thrive.

1881   Paiute Indians from California, Nevada, Oregon, and Washington territory are forced to move to Pyramid Lake Reservation, Malheur River in Oregon, and Fort McDermitt in Nevada.

1889   The second and more prominent phase of the Ghost Dance is founded by Wovoka in Nevada and soon spreads to other tribes. Wovoka had become ill and during this illness had religious visions, again about the revival of traditional ways, lands, resources, and ancestors. This Ghost Dance movement attracts followers among the Great Plains tribes.

1890   US authorities become fearful of the movement's rapid spread and officials try to outlaw the practice.

1890   (Mid-December) US Army officers try to arrest Sitting Bull, a Lakota Shaman and supporter of the Ghost Dance, resulting in a gun battle which kills Sitting Bull. US officers order the arrest of Big Foot, a Lakota chief.

1890   (December 28-29) Big Foot surrenders to US military forces near Wounded Knee Creek. In the process of disarming Lakota men, the US Army opens fire on the camp, killing over 150 Lakota men, women and children.

1891   The massacre at Wounded Knee forces the Ghost Dance movement underground, and in many places it is secret.

1900   The US Department of the Interior orders the arrest of Porcupine, a Cheyenne chief. He is sentenced to hard labor at Fort Keogh for being a leader in the Ghost Dance movement.

1902   Kicking Bear and Short Bull, Sioux Ghost Dance leaders from Pine Ridge Reservation in South Dakota, revive the Ghost Dance on the Fort Belknap and Fort Peck Reservations in Montana.

1915 When an Indian agent learns the identity of Kiowa Ghost Dance leaders, he imprisons them.

1924 Congress grants US citizenship to all Native Americans born in the United States through the Indian Citizenship Act.

1932 Wovoka dies in Yerington, Nevada.

1973 Members of the American Indian Movement (AIM) and Oglala Lakota men and women occupy the trading post at Wounded Knee and do a Ghost Dance ceremony.

Snowshoe Thompson

When Nevada was Utah and gold was king,
first snowfalls cut all communication between Sacramento and Salt Lake.
Torsteinsson left Norway, became Thompson, inched West,
drove milk cows to Placerville, answered ad:
"People Lost to the World; Uncle Sam needs a carrier!"

Carved 10-foot long, 25-pound oak Nordic skis.
Mackinaw jacket, wide-brimmed hat. Charcoaled face
to prevent snow blindness. Rock formations, snow drifts,
tracks and trees his guideposts, stars his navigation points.
90 miles with 100 pounds on his back.

Carried for himself: matches, Bible, dried sausage, crackers.
No blankets, camping gear, compass, or gun.
Carried for others: medicine, clothing, tools, emergency supplies,
books and pans. Needles and lamp chimney so the Widow Franklin
could continue sewing. New strings for the local fiddler.

Saved an isolated man with gangrene.
Carried type case and newsprint for Nevada's first paper.
Took a blue rock to Sacramento. Inside silver. Comstock lode.
20 years of deserted cabins, 80-foot cliffs, grizzlies, lions, and wolves.
Never paid.

In 1978 or 79, I walked clumsily in modern snowshoes
off trail, under pine, my mother in the lead. We traced Thompson's trek
for history and sport. Compass and map, ski gear and sunscreen.
Orienteering the influence of my mother's Norwegian lover,
absent that day.

Now on Horsethief Canyon Trail, I hear the whirl of birds,
the gear shift of semis. I climb boulders, feel red and green lichen,
marvel the soft crunch of dried pine needles.
I recall falling into waist-deep snow, laughing and teetering
between safe and lost.

Green Gold[5]

From Guangdong, South China Sea, Pearl River,
wet road humid ripe with insurrections and incursions.
Through fog banks and Gold Rush
to Great Basin silver.

Gold Canyon and Dayton, Virginia City and Bodie.
Fueled by piñon. Cut by Chinese barred from mining.
Cordwood and charcoal.
English and Hakka, Cantonese and Paiute.

Trade brought small balms. Rice, tea, condiments of home.
Bone-handled toothbrushes, Chinese herbs,
paraphernalia for a body burdened.
Fractures, lost toes, lost fingers, lost lives

in unexpected blizzards. Dougong cabins of willow thatch,
interlocking wood. Men, separated
from wives by law, slept in communal platform beds.
Six spooned for space and warmth.

Chinese tiger whiskey, gin, and five-grain "rice wine."
Dominoes, cards, and dice.
Traveled to Bodie for food and brothels,
Chinese funerals and Chinese New Year.

Levi's overalls, coats sewn with glass beads, fake jade.
For color and luck.
Tea tin, tofu jars, brownware pottery
embossed with "Profit Together" in Chinese.

In Eureka, one found it. All piñon within a 50-mile radius.
750,000 acres cut. Then Exclusion and return.
Boom and bust. Now grass and juniper,
sage and antelope brush.

Smith Valley Haggadah[6]

They arrived, seeking a season of freedom,
crops of grain, trees of fruit.

Lured by lies and desperation
from Austria, Poland, Russia.

Blood and fire and pillars of smoke.
1897. Nevada depression, silver boom bust

welcomed 13 families to Wymore Ranch,
high desert bordered by Pine Nut Mountains,

Buckskin Range, bend of the Walker River.
Orthodox beliefs, collectivist ideals.

Whoever is hungry, let him eat,
and more joined.

Farmers, carpenter, butcher, cobbler, tailor,
blacksmith, wagon maker, rabbi, cantor.

House and barns, tunnels and ditches,
land cleared to farm

alfalfa, wheat, potatoes, hay.
A holy convocation made brief and brutal.

Colony president and secretary mortgaged
crop, absconded with best horses and best wagon.

Those that remained could not pay
to reach families or friends for aid.

We thank you for the land and for the fruit.
Next year in Jerusalem.

Six Weeks[7]

Six weeks, come to take "the cure," break the marriage knot.
High desert air. Clear the mind. Short time, small price.
For freedom. Of a sort.

Six weeks, wedding rings in the Truckee, divorcées on the prowl.
Disillusioned bride clichés for celluloid and vinyl.
Reno, the shorthand. Reno, the punchline.

Six weeks, white women-in-waiting transform
into waitresses and ranch hands, card dealers and clerks.
Sample Virginia Street. Roulette lessons, risqué shows.

Six weeks, Blacks barred from the Mapes and the Riverside,
from dude ranches and motor lodges.
Bills but few work options. Hunger but few eating options.

One Chinese restaurant, Club Harlem, Woolworth's, Bethel AME church socials
Biggest Little City becomes smallest little East Side.
Douglas Alley.

Six weeks, Emma Allen, 23, from Richmond, California,
rents $8-a-week boardinghouse room, referred by Bethel AME.
Ebony Magazine photographs her throwing dice, walking Virginia.

Caption notes Harold's Club has no locks, doors always open.
Does not mention Emma could not enter. Casinos hang signs
"No Indians, Negroes, or Dogs."

Six weeks, Emma hires white lawyer. Shops for groceries.
Meets local NAACP leader. Says, Reno is in the Dark Ages.
Says it will be pleasant when she gets back home. Waits. For freedom.

The Meadows (Las Vegas)

Once it was not ironic—wild grasses and desert,
cottonwoods and mesquite bosques,
fresh water and frogs, grassy beaver meadows.

Here water broke through barren with such force
Paiute swimmers could not dive under
"Bubbling Sand Spring."

In 1829 a trader from Mexico trekked the Old Spanish Trail
with 60 men, blankets and goods to trade for mules,
Santa Fe to Los Angeles,

sent scout to find water. On the Epiphany, when the magi
are said to have brought gifts from other lands
to a newborn Jesus—gold, frankincense, myrrh—

king, god, and death—men searched for the scout,
found Yerba del Manso Arroyo, the mouth of the Las Vegas Wash,
just above where Hoover Dam would change the fate

of men and meadows. Twenty miles west, in the bubbling sand,
traders, immigrants, and gold diggers drank, hunted, and met.
Goats, cows, and mules slaked their thirst.

Settlers built pipelines and dams, private wells and roads,
utility corridors and dumping sites until the last water rose
to wet the ground in 1962.

Irrigation was introduced. Life support for a half-mile
of creek remains. Now from the spring mound, one can see
the Strip—neon-soaked fever dream six miles away—

and the Bellagio, in Paradise, Nevada, where eight acres
of fountains pump millions of gallons of water each day
from a freshwater well.

Miss Atomic Blast

1951 Vegas was young, small, and ignorant,
if not innocent. Six hotels on the Strip, Sinatra debuted
at the Desert Inn, and the Nevada Test Site became a spectacle.
Calendars were given with detonation times, best places to watch.
Showgirls and singers, craps and blasts—who could ask for anything more?

Atomic cocktails and penthouse views, sunglasses and souvenirs,
toys and candies. "Dawn bomb parties" to revel in the lighting of a night sky.
A Sands chorus girl danced on Angel's Peak as test cloud bloomed behind.
Her poses named "apprehension" and "impact," "awe" and "survival."
Tests were named Annie and Priscilla, Hornet and Bee.

At the El Rancho, a young dancer was crowned Miss Atomic Blast,
awarded 10 pounds of mushrooms.
In 1957, another showgirl won Miss Atomic Bomb.
Icon of blond curls, red lips,
white bikini with cotton mushroom from hips to chin.

Flash blinded sheep, Joshua trees smoldered, burns killed livestock,
but general said the worst was a "mouthful of dirt." The government said
no danger outside the bombing range. 41 years, 928 tests.
Soldiers who witnessed were more likely to die from leukemia,
prostate and throat cancers.

And now, as fans of TV's "Chernobyl" rush to relish its devastation,
the US Department of Energy offers tours of the Nevada site, calls Sedan Crater,
"The perfect place for a group photo." The pit created by 104-kiloton device,
635 feet underground. Radiation signs hang from wire fences.
The tour is booked out for a year.

Prometheus Felled[8]

Bristlecone twist upon twist, layer upon layer, like fingers
of the crone or braids of her mother, reaching for the sky.
Cold air, hot sun. High desert survivor

dared erosions and fires, needed only a few small strips
of bark to stay alive, outlive them all.
But 5,000 years were undone in one afternoon.

We want to know, to name.
We are Machiavellian in this pursuit.
Prometheus stole fire from the gods, carried it

in giant fennel stalk, gifted it to humans.
For this, he was bound to a rock, his liver to be eagle-eaten
every day, regrow at night and be eaten again.

To understand the brain's hemispheres, we cut the corpus collosum.
To learn the spread of virus, we cull the herd, open skulls.
To know the oldest, we bored the bark,

failed, then cut and sectioned, hauled and processed.
Counted rings, counted time. Only then did we understand
the ignorance and arrogance.

Still, we kept one slab at Ely casino, then convention center.
Respect reserved for the lab or the field. Now national park
in part because scientist-cum-lumberjack pushed

to protect remaining pine, hobble the folly
of men, like him, believing they need to know,
no matter the damnation, no matter the pain.

Dusty Spurs

The Bicentennial. Celebrations helped find a way out from Vietnam, from Waterga
We painted fire hydrants on 7th Street. Dodged fireworks. Sang Elton John and Kiki D
Biggest Little City decked in red, white, and blue. Stars and stripes. And chaps.

For his vision, Phil Ragsdale needed livestock. Asked farmers and ranchers.
Three dozen refused. Before one said Yes. Five cows, ten calves, one pig, one Shetland po
The night before the first Gay Rodeo.

150 attended. Fundraiser for senior citizens. Winners crowned
King of Cowboys, Queen of Cowgirls, Miss Dusty Spurs. Word spread through We
Strong men. Holding hands, riding broncos. Bandanas in pockets.

Codes and community. Rodeo grew, drew more. Men, women, genderqueer.
The love of Country and Western. Horses and pride. Protests began in parking lo
Lieutenant Governor opposed 7,000 "queers" using public property,

Said "it's unnatural." Letter to editor said "termites…brazenly oozed out
of their closet." But still they came. 1982. Washoe County Fairgrounds. 20,000 in stan
Over $35,000 raised. Joan Rivers was Grand Marshal. Theme was Western Gay Prid

We listened to Joan Jett, Soft Cell. Thought Rodeo would go on forever. Was as Re
as Harold's Club and Mapes Hotel, Bertha and Tina (John Ascuaga's elephants
Then *Los Angeles Times* cover story said mysterious fever, now epidemic.

1983. 7,500 signed petition to ban Rodeo. Three TV stations received threats.
Said snipers poised to shoot attendees. ACLU debated Christian-Coalition. Only 12,C
attend. The others went inside. Rallied around each other. Supported the dying. Comfc

Survivors. Became family. The final National Reno Gay Rodeo 1984.
10,000 people came to fairgrounds. The first person I know contracted HIV.
(Though it would be another four years before we knew.)

Fight, family, fun. The end was the start. Gay Rodeo Association went
international. Over 500 rodeos held. Denver to Baltimore. Omaha to Calgary. Ren
Bull riding, steer wrestling. Calf roping, barrel racing. Wild Drag Race.

Items Left After Burning Man

Cellphones, IDs, bags, suitcases,
shirts, jackets, hydration backpacks,

eyeglasses, a partial pair of dentures,
water bottles, a wedding ring,

a flute, a piano tuning kit, a marching band hat,
a stuffed bunny, a furry cheetah vest, a stuffed cow,

single sandals, chainmail skirt, the fuselage of a Boeing 747,
100 gallons of oil, grey water, black water,

800,000 gallons of wastewater,
oxidized decomposed granite, burn scars.

OREGON

Oregon State Timeline

1843   First white settlers convene "wolf meetings" to deal with problem of wolves menacing their settlements.

1844   Elijah White, Oregon Territory's resident Indian agent, recommends that Blacks be banned from Oregon as "dangerous subjects."

1844   First statement of public policy by US settlers to exclude Blacks passes in Territory, punishing any Blacks who try to settle in Oregon with 39 lashes repeated every six months until they leave. (This is later changed to forced labor. In 1845, the policy is repealed.)

1847   13 whites killed by members of the Cayuse tribe near Walla Walla (then part of the Oregon Territory).

1849   Oregon Territorial legislature enacts laws prohibiting a "Negro or mulatto to enter into or reside within the limits of the Territory."

1849   White resident in Linn City launches arson attack on a Native American village, destroying their winter provisions.

1849   New law declares it would be "highly dangerous to allow free Negroes and mulattoes to reside in the Territory or to intermix with Indians, instilling into their minds feelings of hostility toward the white race."

1850–54   US Congress passes Donation Land Act giving 320 or 640 acres in Oregon for free to whites and "half-breed Indians."

1850   Jacob Vanderpool, a Black sailor from the West Indies, arrives in Oregon City and begins operating a boarding house.

1851   Vanderpool is arrested, convicted of violating the Exclusion Act for the crime of "being Black in Oregon," and ordered to be removed from Oregon within 30 days.

1857   US Supreme Court decides Dred Scott case. The Court holds that the US Constitution was not meant to include citizenship for Blacks (free or enslaved), and thus, the rights and privileges of citizens do not apply to them. The decision also affirms the right of slave owners to take slaves into Western territories.

1857   Oregon's Constitution bans Blacks from living, working, owning property, or voting in the state.

1859   Oregon admitted as US state. The only state admitted with an exclusionary clause.

1862   The Homestead Act provides any adult citizen, or intended citizen, who had never fought against the US government, with 160 acres of surveyed government land in the West.

1862   New Oregon law requires all Blacks, Chinese, native Hawai'ians, and multiracial people to pay a $5 annual tax.

1862   Oregon adopts an anti-miscegenation law, prohibiting whites from marrying anyone who is Chinese, native Hawai'ian, or ¼ or more Black.

1866   Oregon Legislature bans all marriages between members of different racial groups.

1866   The Oregon legislature ratifies the 14th Amendment by a narrow margin.

1868   14th Amendment ratified and adopted into the Constitution, granting citizenship and equal civil and legal rights to Blacks and emancipated slaves.

1868   Elections bring the Democrats into power in Oregon. They promptly rescind the state's ratification of the 14th Amendment, despite the Amendment having just become federal law.

1870   15th Amendment ratified, granting legal voting rights to Black men. (Literacy tests and other measures will restrict the ability of all Black men to exercise their right to vote.)

1900   Oregon voters reject taking exclusionary clause out of the state constitution, even though it no longer holds any legal power due to the 14th Amendment.

1921   KKK organizes chapter in Oregon.

1923   Walter Pierce, with active support from the KKK, becomes governor.

1923   Alien Land Act bars immigrants from owning or renting land (passed with only one dissenting vote) and bans immigrants from operating hospitality businesses in effort to thwart Japanese and Chinese immigration.

1926   Exclusion clause taken out of Oregon's constitution.

1927   State constitution amended to remove voting restrictions against Blacks and Chinese Americans.

1951   Oregon's anti-miscegenation law is rescinded.

1959   Oregon ratifies the 15th Amendment, 91 years after the US adopted it.

1973   Oregon re-ratifies the 14th Amendment, 103 years after the US adopted it.

1988   Ethiopian immigrant Mulugeta Seraw fatally beaten by three white supremacists in Portland.

2002   Racist language in state constitution removed.

2017   Two people fatally stabbed and a third injured on a Portland light rail train by a white supremacist shouting anti-Muslim slurs against two teenage girls.

Crater Lake[9]

Men would swim at night, meet Llao,
spirit of the Below World, imprisoned in the water,
earn their vision, prove their bravery.
One man lost his child, dove underneath, begged,
"Give me power, catch me." He emerged a shaman.

Others would camp by crater,
pile rocks, break twigs, tie together,
pile rocks, break twigs, tie together until
dawn brought sleep and dreams of bear
or wolf, coyote or skunk or birds. Medicine.

One man, white and in love before he ever saw
the lake, did not fear or seek inside. Proud, he wanted
to share his beloved with the world, like a king
who parades his young bride before his people,
pulling her from her kin, creating resentments
inside that will ultimately alter her beauty.

He became its superintendent. Caretaking
gave way to hubris. He built roads and trails,
phone and water systems, wanted more.
Wanted a road inside crater, an elevator
to lakeshore, a bridge to Wizard Island.
Was ousted after three years.

On pilgrimages to our extended family's homes,
we would pass and ignore the signs pointing east.
Two times for Christmas, two times for summer,
two times, two times. Still young enough to feel
the pull of family, the push to find
my own path.

Once, in my 20s, alone, I paused before the moonscape,
fought the urge to feel how warm the water,
to dive and ask, "untie my eyes."
Now I want to pile and break and tie,
to dive and sleep and learn
my medicine as I sit in isolation, waiting
for an unseen pandemic curve to flatten,
for Llao to be appeased.

Madame Governor[10]

For 48 hours and 55 minutes,
years before she had the right,
she had the power.

At 16, full of young state tragedy, Carrie Bertha Shelton
married a judge, her guardian. Widowed at 18,
she trusted her mind, became stenographer,

learned the work of male lawyers, prepared deeds and mortgages,
made her mark. Followed her boss to district attorney's office,
drafted criminal indictments. Followed Chamberlain again

to governor's office, broke ground as personal secretary,
helped him become senator, unaware what it meant for us.
In 1908, Oregonian men voted down women's suffrage. Months later,

Carrie would take office. Chamberlain resigned to go to DC. Secretary of State
too ill to be sworn in. Constitution left Carrie. Nation's first female governor.
She could issue pardons, veto bills, sign executive orders,

but not cast her own ballot. Carrie again joined Chamberlain,
oversaw staff in Washington. And on November 5, 1912, she celebrated
Wilson's victory and won the right to vote in Oregon.

She married Chamberlain in 1926. Her obituary,
with its wrong date and her unofficial name, mentioned his time
as governor, but never hers.

Kirpan

"Brave Hindis! Awaken from your sleep."
—Ghadar Party Statement 1914

They fled fertile, alluvial plains. A flood of pain from plague, protests,
and early partitions. Punjabi Muslims, Hindus, Sikhs, mostly Sikhs streamed
into area bordered by the Columbia and the Willamette, flush with pine and fir.
Labored in lumber, sheltered in company bunkhouses, shared apartments downtown.
Tried to plant roots in a new town built on the felling of old trees.

Spring equinox 1910, violence began with the smash of beer against brown skin.
Mayor, police chief, officers, the sweetshop's son, 200 others joined. Marched
to the homes of "dusky-skinned natives," broke in, threw out,
forced them onto Portland-bound trains. Looted, vandalized, then slept.
Clothing scattered, doors off hinges, blood on dirt.

Sikhs have five items of faith. Uncut hair, wooden comb, iron bracelet, cotton
undergarment, iron dagger. *Kesh, kangha, kara, kachera, kirpan.* "Kirpa" and "aan."
Mercy and dignity. Knives tucked in. Never used. Perhaps they wondered why
mercy is the onus of the victim. Perhaps they saw a chance to carve something new.
Double-edged. Less than, more than. British Indian subjects.

Kanshi Ram, a dozen more, went to consulate, returned
with Deputy District Attorney, walked streets, pointed out their attackers.
200 warrants, multiple trials, two convictions, one inspiration. Dignity.
Early March 1912, in Portland house Kanshi Ram and Sohan Singh Bhakna gathered
Indian immigrants to overthrow British Raj. Mutiny. Ghadar. Revolt.

The People's Champion

September 14, 1911. 12,000 people witnessed saddle bronc final and
history in small eastern Oregon ranch town. West's best riders.
Three men. Three biographies. Brown, White, and Black.

Jackson Sundown, middle-aged nephew of Nez Perce Chief Joseph.
John A. Spain, Oregon son of white "pioneers."
George Fletcher, African-American, came to Oregon as a child.

Sundown born Waaya-Tonah-Toesits-Kahn, Blanket of the Sun, Nez Perce
and Salish cowboy. At 14, forced north with tribe. Joined exiled Sitting Bull and Siou
in Canada, became breeder and breaker of horses. Adopted new name for rodeo

Sundown knew the power of spectacle. At 48, six-foot-tall, long braids tied under chin
wide brim hat wrapped with silk scarf, beaded gauntlets, spotted wooly chaps.
Rodeo circuit legend. Scared competition from entering.

Spain, Oregonian son of Nebraska farmers. Fled abusive father. Saw Buffalo Bill
Wild West, vowed to become showman. Earned enough bucking broncs to buy ranc
create pageant. Four-horse chariots, hippodrome races. "Last of the Real Wild West Shows

By 1910, Umatilla County Sheriff Tillman Taylor founded competition.
Pendleton Round-Up. Wanted Spain's bucking stock.
Invited Spain to compete.

Fletcher, Kansas-born, as young boy came to a state that did not want him,
that taxed and exiled Blacks for the crime of being in Oregon. Pendleton public schoo
slurs and attacks. Moved to mission school, Umatilla Reservation. Learned languag

customs and horsemanship. Practiced bucking on barrels. First rodeo at 12. Bulls an
buffalo. He and another rider on same horse, same saddle, opposite directions.
Third place at District Fair. Only African-American in first Pendleton Round-U

In 1911. Three men. Four horses. No eight-second rule. Sundown first.
Rode Lightfoot. 25 seconds. Horse tried to bite his leg, ran into judges' mount,
threw Sundown to ground. Knocked unconscious. Disqualified. No re-ride.

Spain rode Long Tom. Broke through fence. Showman stuck.
But some cried foul. Said he grabbed leather, touched horse
with free hand.

Fletcher first rode Del. Horse refused to buck. Crowd demanded new horse.
Loose and limber, "like rubber band," Fletcher stayed on. Clean.
But Spain crowned champion, awarded silver-trimmed saddle.

Crowd cried foul again. Sheriff Til grabbed own hat, cut it into pieces,
sold each scrap for $5, turned $700 over to Fletcher. Double the saddle's worth.
Declared him the "People's Champion."

Fire Balloon (Fu-Go)[11]

Bulbs, rubberized silk or paper,
and 19,000 cubic feet of hydrogen rose in the Empire,
swayed with the jet stream, floated among the birds.

On the Weyerhaeuser Timber Company's property
in southern Oregon, far from the Pacific and European theaters,
three days after the German surrender,

two months after the fire bombs in Tokyo, a pastor
pulled over, let out five young teens, his pregnant wife,
her unborn child pressed against her bladder

or perhaps morning sickness rose to her throat.
The six wandered into the high desert forest of fir and pine,
aspen and wildflowers in bloom this May in 1945.

He stayed, spoke to a construction crew about fishing—
the streams rich with rainbow and brook trout,
the woods with deer, black bear, and mountain lion.

"Look what I found, dear," she called before she knew
her fate—dress on fire, dead branches and dust, bodies strewn,
the chocolate cake left untouched in the car.

The pastor, his ability to speak to strangers his survival
and his downfall, was left to mourn in the prescribed
silence of military secrets and knowledge of an enemy's reach.

They could not know their success, we could not know
how much there was to fear. And as the world
prepared to lose any innocence it had left that August,

the pastor sought refuge in his faith. Later, he would find new love, leave
to spread the good word to the souls of Vietnam, only to be captured
at the leprosarium by the Viet Cong, never to be found again.

Shevlin[12]

Oregon high desert homesteads. Virgin ponderosa
waiting to be ravaged. Blessed are the Sitka spruce, Douglas fir
that make their cutters work. They will stay longer in the earth.

Shevlin-Hixon. Hunger deep, demanding. More. Each acre felled. More.
Scandinavian bachelors axed until sun touched ground. Boxcar bunkhouses
lifted and loaded onto rails. South to new forest. Fast pace, clear cut.

Lumber boom. Wives and children. Porches that folded.
Roads bulldozed and left, latrines built and covered. Cookhouse,
bath house. Postmaster, barber, tavern, school. All lifted and loaded.

A moveable town. No replanting of people or pine. By 1950, 200,000 acres
hewn. Shelvin sold. But in 1920, company had donated 1,000 acres for city park.
Half century later, we would gather under those pines. Generations of men

who worked the mills, their family and friends. We ate potato salad, drank soda,
played horseshoe. The youngest of us collected creek rocks, climbed trees.
Listened to the woodpecker, the drumming of the ruffed grouse.

Truth and Mercy

"What more can any man ask than to have been on the side of life and truth and beauty, to have played his part honorably and as well as his talents allowed, and to have loved mercy and done justly?"
—Dr. Alan L. Hart

1890   Alan Hart is named "Alberta" by his parents at birth.[13]
He would grow to follow his grandfather, play Civil War games,
love pocketknives, chopping wood. In the shade of Western Cascades.

> Two men are sent to Oregon Penitentiary for "Sodomy!",
> notes clerk who does not add emphasis to men
> convicted for rape or manslaughter.

1902   Hart family moves, Hart child grows. Must present as female.
Relief upon return to Linn County, grandparents and farm.
Free to tease girls, play among boys.

1917   Hart graduates medical school. Bittersweet trophy.
First person enrolled as a woman to receive medal
for highest standing in all departments.
That winter, becomes man.
Finds doctor who sees him, frees him.
Alan changes his name, marries his first wife.
Sets up medical practice in Gardiner, near the Umpqua River.

> Oregon legislature passes law to sterilize
> "sexual perverts" and "moral degenerates."

1935   Hart develops X-ray tool for early tuberculosis diagnosis.
Screens thousands. Cuts Idaho's death-rate by four-fifths.
Publishes first novel, *Doctor Mallory*.
Exposes greed, prejudice in medicine.
Celebrates tenth anniversary with second wife.

> Oregon governor requires a list of "sexual perverts"
> be turned over to Board of Eugenics for possible sterilization,
> crime committed or not.

1943   Hart compiles evidence. X-rays to detect TB, other conditions.
        Writes the book. *These Mysterious Rays*. Still standard text.
        Saves countless lives.

1948   Hart becomes a director at Connecticut TB Commission.
        Contains spread in state. Other states follow.
        Official photo—tweed jacket, wooden pipe,
        slicked short hair, wire-rim glasses.
        Confidence.

1953   Oregon passes psychopathic offender law.
                Those convicted of sodomy, even if consensual,
                could receive life sentence.

1957   Hart raises funds for medical research, support for poorer patients.

                Oregon prohibits anyone convicted of sodomy
                from becoming a public school teacher.

1962   An Oregon legislative committee investigating
                "social problems" learns Oregon State Hospital
                recently fired several lesbian employees.

        Hart dies of heart failure. Ashes scattered over Puget Sound.
        His wife lives 20 more years. Their estate funds research
        for leukemia and other diseases, notes
        Hart was "devoted to medicine."

Ghost Forest[14]

In the time before, Thunderbird flapped his wings,
   brought storms and rain, fought Whale under ocean,
     above fog. Caused waters to rise, woods to tremble,
       earth to fall, man to speak this battle into generations

of bands silenced into another history
   that forgot waves tall as spruce and redwood,
     coasts pulled into sand, remnants of cedar and Sitka
       left to shade salmon and albacore, sturgeon and perch.

In the time of now, El Niño arrives like prophet,
   drags water back like blanket to reveal sentinels.
     Roots and stumps rise like fingers to pull body, grab sky,
       sound the sirens as Thunderbird and Whale prepare for battle.

Items From Japan Found on Oregon's Coasts
Since the 2011 Japanese Tsunami

Plastics, floats, foams.
Buoys, pilings, propane tank.
Tubes, tires, shoes, and children's toys.

Broom handle, dustpan, dishrack, tray.
Buckets, baskets, bowls, bottle caps.
Jugs, rope, and sieve.

Spruce, fir, and Japanese black pine.
Logs, crates, pallets, barrel fragments, boards.
At least 26 boats and a 188-ton, 66-foot concrete dock.

Asian amur sea star,
Japanese yellowtail jack, Asian shore crab,
the invasive seaweed Undaria pinnatifida.

Over 280 species of sponges, mussels, barnacles, limpets,
sea slugs, sea anemones, amphipods, and fish.
84 species of marine algae and cyanobacteria.

WASHINGTON

Grand Coulee Dam Timeline

Prior to mid-1800s   Columbia Basin supports an estimated 7-30 million salmon and steelhead.

1900   There are an estimated 10-16 million anadromous fish runs annually in the Columbia River.

1902   Reclamation Act gives the US Reclamation Service the ability to initiate large-scale projects in the West.

1914   Washington voters reject a $40-million bond issue to finance a series of pumping stations to siphon water from the Columbia at the Grand Coulee.

1917   Attorney Bill Clapp from the Columbia Basin town of Ephrata begins discussing the idea of a large dam to provide irrigation to the region. Rufus Woods, influential publisher of the *Wenatchee World* newspaper, goes on to relentlessly promote this idea in his paper.

1928   Anthropologist Verne Ray begins doing field work on the Colville Reservation. He notes that every household he visited offered him salmon as part of the meal.

1932   Preliminary permit is issued to the state. The Confederated Tribes of the Colville Reservation protest.

1933-36 The Columbia Basin Commission surveys and appraises land needed for the creation of Lake Roosevelt.

1933   President Franklin Roosevelt promises federal support for the Grand Coulee Dam as part of the New Deal. Later that year, groundbreaking ceremonies are held, days before funds are approved for the Bonneville Dam, another dam downstream on the Columbia.

1934   President Franklin Roosevelt visits the construction site. As the dam will lead to the breakup of private utility monopolies, Roosevelt touts that electricity will be made "so cheap that it will become a standard article of use not only for manufacturing but for every home."

1934   Mason City built to house workers. Other towns, including Engineers Town, are built by the Reclamation Service.

1935   Concrete placement begins. Nearly 11,000 men work over 27 million hours to divert the Columbia River, excavate the foundation, and place concrete. Forty-five men die in the process.

1936   Land for Lake Roosevelt scheduled to be taken at year's end. Reclamation Service does not assist in the resettlement of families and towns.

1937   Lake Roosevelt begins forming when the dam's foundation is spanned.

1938   The Grand Coulee Dam cuts off the upper Columbia River for migrating anadromous fish. The dam blocks all anadromous fish runs to Spokane, Coeur d'Alene, Kalispel, and Kootenai Reservations and traditional off-reservation fishing locations.

1939   Rising reservoir levels inundate the first town, the tribal town of Keller. The town is subsequently moved several times.

1939-40 Members of the Colville and Spokane tribes whose land was to be flooded are notified. However, there is no formal process of involving tribes in decision-making or in obtaining consent for the land.

1939   Reclamation Service contracted for the reopening, removal, and reburial of graves at 27 sites along the Columbia and Spokane Rivers. Some gravesites are left to be flooded.

1940   Water covers all 54 of the first tracts, but the federal government has acquired deeds to only 43. No owner is financially compensated.

1941   Indians from throughout the Northwest gather at Kettle Falls for a three-day "Ceremony of Tears," mourning the loss of fishing grounds. Within the month, the rising reservoir covers the falls.

1941   First power is generated at Grand Coulee power plant.

1941-1945 Power from Grand Coulee is essential in the manufacture of wartime aluminum for the construction of warships in Portland and Boeing warplanes in Seattle and also in the manufacture of plutonium at Hanford Site nuclear production complex. Plutonium from the Hanford Site is used in the first nuclear bomb and in the third bomb detonated over Nagasaki, Japan.

1948 Water pumped from the dam begins reaching the Columbia Basin.

1967 Construction begins on a third power plant. The dam is the largest hydropower producer in the US.

1978 The Indian Claims Commission awards more than $3 million for the subsistence value of fish lost to the claimant tribes since 1940.

1980 The 1980 Northwest Power Act mandates the protection, mitigation, and enhancement of habitat losses from hydropower development and provides for the active involvement of tribes.

1989 Consideration of wildlife is amended into the Act.

1995 The federal government compensates the Confederated Colville Tribes a $53 million lump sum and an annual payment of at least $15 million for the unfulfilled agreement from 1933 to pay the tribes an annual share of power revenues.

2000 There are an estimated 2.5 million anadromous fish runs annually in the Columbia River.

Mid-2000s Cheap power from the Grand Coulee and other dams along the Columbia River attracts "server farms" from Amazon, Microsoft, and Google to the Columbia Basin.

Los Mozos Arrieros (The Young Muleteers)[15]

I want to know the songs of men silent
save the tinkling of mare's bell, the calls
of *hippah* and *mulah*, the rhythm of hoofs and feet
in the stillness of pine and redwood.

I want to know the songs of men silent,
paid in gold, tracked by thieves.
Lift and load, cook and mend,
diamond hitch *aparejo*, rifles in their hands.

I want to know the songs of men silent
from our stories of mines and Manifest,
who fed Walla Walla to Boise, through cliffs
and canyons, with whiskey, iron, casket, spice.

The Tacoma Method

By the rails, by the mill, at the head of the Puget Sound, Little Canton
grew. Pastel paper curtains and bamboo furniture, narrow gardens
and temples with joss sticks, stores that sold porcelain and rice, teas and silks.
Men who worked canneries and lumber camps, saw mills and coal mines.

February 1885, Chinese and white merchants celebrated Lunar New Year
together. *Gong Hei Fat Choy*, Congratulations and be prosperous.
You have escaped the harm of Nian, the mountain beast that eats
everything in its path. They spoke too soon.

That month, mayor said all Chinese must go. Come November,
500 angry whites, including mayor, including police, gathered
and marched down by the rails, by the mill. Went door to door, secure
in their anger. Pulled children and elders from homes, businesses.

Gave orders to leave, forced 200 to walk eight miles to board trains
that went on tracks the Chinese helped build. Then, like Nian,
they ate everything in their path, setting Little Canton on fire.
Fire department defended rail timbers, let Chinatown burn.

On the day that 27 were indicted, including mayor and fire chief,
a local German club threw a gala in their honor. They were cheered
en route to trial, welcomed back with a band and parties
as heroes, never convicted.

One white resident praised the pogrom, said it was common practice to expel
a community that "ceased to be useful and had become…inconvenient."
Dubbed it "The Tacoma Method," said it would "go far to immortalize
the pleasant city." Nian, I learn, has no shame.

Call of the Timberbeasts

CHORUS

They tried to silence loggers and miners,
limit growing labor agitation,
ban speaking on streets.[16]

Never ignore your heroes.
You create a roadmap for resistance.

But the bindlestiffs, timberbeasts, and "unkempt Ciceros"
each climbed a soapbox,
were berated, beaten, and brought to jail.

Never test a man well past hunger.
He will fight for his right to beg.

Thirty days inside prison, abandoned school, or barracks,
sweat boxes then ice-cold cells, soft pine for pillows, hard floor for beds,
they worked the rock pile, ate only bread and water, fell ill.

Ideas survive the burning of papers,
the killing of men.

Rebel girl, all of 19, chained herself to a post,
served time, published accounts of jail conditions, police brutality,
of men in court matted with blood, women's section used as brothel.

Never underestimate the capacity of shame
to change minds or at least open cells.

Five months after first box smashed, after 500 arrested and three dead,
the city council found its way to freedoms already enshrined,
and the unheard alone found power united.

George Washington once warned the Army,
"The freedom of Speech may be taken away and, dumb & silent,
we may be led, like sheep, to the Slaughter."

The Fourth[17]

When threatened, overwhelmed, we are quick
to trade liberty for order amid chaos.
Cut our nose to spite our rights.

World War I, Wilson declared, "the world must be safe for democracy."
But the United States is always exceptional.
Here, an ad exec can create

the American Protective League. Vigilante, volunteer.
Counterintelligence. No training, no selection, no oversight.
Justice Department approval. Fake badges. Real guns.

Sought and saw German sympathizers—rough code for pacifists,
labor unions, African-Americans, immigrants, uppity women.
Allegations and arrests. Raids and surveillance.

Wilson wrote concerns to Attorney General, left his inaction to history.
No limits, no end. Seattle APL boasted 11,000 members,
files on thousands more. Spies on the waterfront,

spies at the shipyard. Disloyalty assumed, strikes disrupted, men detained.
Six months in 1918, 1,008 arrest made.
Cases investigated: 1,198 Industrial Workers of the World agitators,

707 loyalty reports, 451 alleged spies or German agents,
449 seditious utterances, 64 liquor sales to soldiers and sailors.
Fear. Power. Profusion. 250,000 members in 600 cities.

Peace killed purpose. New AG stopped APL affiliation.
Warned such actions could harm the probably innocent.
Now, as Seattle streets mourn George Floyd, Breonna Taylor, Ahmaud Arbery,

militia members anoint themselves "peacekeepers," carry zip ties, shoot paintballs
One holds his .45 caliber, says it is time to act.
White House turns a seeing eye.

Emerald City

1931. Before we knew how close the edge. A tent became
a village, became a city. Scandinavian and Filipino,
African-American and Mexican. Nine acres, 500 self-built houses,
1,200 men, seven women. Shipyard Hooverville.

Breadlines and "bumming." Odd jobs and full-time.
Lumber, rail, highways, bridges, mines. Cannery workers and
farm laborers, fishermen and newsboys. Schoolteacher.
Rat walks to toilets, gas cans for water.

Houses of wood. Old boxes for chairs. Kerosene
to heat, to cook, and twice to burn the village down.
Police at dawn. Lit torches. Caught like tinder.
Rebuilt with tin and concrete. Determination born of desperation.

Vigilante committee patrolled. Two whites, two Blacks, two Filipinos.
Kept the constant pain from overflowing, destroying what was left.
Cold, hunger, depression, suicide.
Soot on walls, soot on food, soot in lungs.

Once some men picked blackberries from Beacon Hill,
made blackberry jam. Sweetened the sour soot and soul.
Better than the city shelters. Better than the outside.
Dignity and community. Agency and autonomy.

Now police and field coordinators clear tent cities that sprout
under freeways, on streets. Desperation. Determination.
Now 300 tiny houses built. Restrooms and showers. Kitchens and
case managers. For 11,000 without homes. 5,000 without shelter.

Boeing Wonderland[18]

Years before Levittown, Hollywood was called in
to sell American dream to Japanese pilots who never came.

Plywood and clapboard, chicken wire and burlap,
camouflage, feathers, and spun glass. Real grass and real weeds.

"Synthetic Street" and "Burlap Boulevard," wink and nod.
Houses too small, streets too quiet.

26 acres of fantasy above factory hid thousands of women,
thousands of men, thousands of new bombs.

Then infamy and fear exchanged roles. Victim became hunter.
Months after firebombing Tokyo, contract to dismantle the farce.

Weeks before Nagasaki and Hiroshima, publicity photos released.
Young white women in fitted suits or short skirts and bikini tops,

hair coifed—nary a uniform, hardly a man—enjoying ersatz
breaks, sunbathing, strolling, chatting where just before,

they could not go. Celebrating successful lies through more
deception. The great rehearsal for a suburban swell.

At the Midnite Mine[19]

Twin brothers uncovered the glow
where the Spokane and Columbia rivers meet

on discarded land too rough to plow.
Cold War, hot rocks, patriotism, pride.

Through town to mill, crush and beat,
patty-cake, yellowcake, paycheck, man.

Miners brought home playthings:
hard rubber balls, pretty green rocks,

dust beneath trucks, dust in the air,
dusty work clothes washed off-site.

Near the pit, women tanned deer and elk hides.
Sweat lodges had tainted willow and water.

Young man swam in the river, ate
roots and berries and wild game.

Died of a rot that started in his bladder,
spread through his limbs.

Volunteer gravedigger, worked the mine,
blesses too many plots with sage and sweetgrass.

Thought he was providing for the family
he contaminated every day.

Spokane Falls

Along the Falls, along the River, gathered salmon and men.
Once, one million summer chinooks spawned in the waters,
the Spokane made fishing camps, sun-dried and smoked to last through winter.

By the time my family came, whites had sacrificed salmon for sawmills, flour mills
generators, railroads. Dams and wood chips. Sewage and PCBs.
Warehouses obscured the River, elevated rails drowned

the rush of Falls. My father worked at a brewery, but wouldn't drink the beer.
The water soured the taste. Inevitable flight to suburbs, to the new.
Urban renewal meant finding a way back to the flow.

In 1974 Spokane would host first eco-world's fair.
Trestles removed, river opened, gondola built.
Amid Watergate, Nixon stood on float in the middle of the River,

said the expo would leave a legacy. New park, new spirit, new habitat.
On opening day, 1,974 rainbow trout were released into the water,
1,000 pigeons into the sky.

One year later, in the fall of 1975, my uncle, soft-spoken, so full of love
and patience for five-year-old me, joined the fresh rush of water over rocks,
the vibrancy that shouted life itself.

Items in the Remains of the 1980 Mount St. Helens Eruption

4 billion board feet of timber, standing dead forest,
wheat and apple crops, potato and alfalfa crops,
68,000 acres of Weyerhaeuser timber farm.

200 houses. Camps and cabins.
Stoves and refrigerators.
Doorway with "No Smoking" sign.

47 bridges, 15 miles of railways, 185 miles of highway,
cars, trailers, semis flipped over, bull dozers, fuel tanks,
logging truck with trees growing out its middle.

5,000 deer, 1,500 elk, 40,000 young salmon,
12 million salmon, millions of birds, 57 people,
including the unseen remains of 83-year-old Harry R. Truman
who refused to leave his Spirit Lake Lodge.

Notes

1. The Salmon River is a 19.6-mile-long (31.5 km) tributary to the Klamath River in western Siskiyou County, California, near the Oregon border. My family had mining claims in this region. This timeline reflects primarily the recorded settler history.

2. Inspired by "The Long, Long Trail to '49: Personal Memories of Remembrance Campbell," *The Morning Union*, December 11, 1923 (Nevada City, CA), and the personal writings of Remembrance Campbell.

3. Hercules, California began as a company town of California Powder Works, later Hercules Powder Works, named for "Hercules powder," a specially patented formulation of dynamite. The majority of its employees were Chinese immigrants and Chinese-Americans.

4. On April 7, 2016, Luís Góngora Pat, a 45-year-old man from the Mayan village of Teabo, in the Mexican province of Yucatán, was shot by two police officers. Within 30 seconds of exiting their patrol vehicles, San Francisco Police Department's officers unloaded five beanbag rounds and seven live rounds at Luís. According to all witness accounts, Luis was sitting on the ground by himself, minding his own business, when the officers launched an unmerited attack and killed him.

5. The poem was informed by the "Fueling the Boom: Chinese Woodcutters in the Great Basin 1870-1920" exhibit at the Nevada State Museum. The exhibit highlighted the significance of the woodcutting community near Chinese Camp (Aurora), Nevada. Chinese woodcutters who lived there felled piñon (or pinyon) pines to supply charcoal and firewood to the mining camps of Bodie and Aurora from approximately 1875 to 1915.

6. In the late 1890s, the Hebrew Agricultural Society of the United States unveiled a plan to triple Nevada's population with thousands of Eastern European Jews. In 1897, Governor Reinhold Sadler commissioned Jewish entrepreneurs Morris Cohn and Theodore Hofer to take out an option on 5,500-acres in Wellington. The collectivist

arrangement was that each family would own a house and some private property. They would all share ownership and production of the remaining land. In October, 17 families signed deeds and 62 colonists traveled to Wellington, with 12 more families to follow.

7. From 1906 until the late 1960s, Reno was the "Divorce Capital of the World." Before no-fault divorces were the norm, Nevada offered relatively quick divorces, provided those seeking a divorce fulfilled a residency requirement of six weeks.

8. Prometheus, a Great Basin bristlecone pine recorded as WPN-114, was the oldest known non-clonal organism. It was growing near the tree line on Wheeler Peak in eastern Nevada before it was cut down for research purposes in 1964 by a graduate student and United States Forest Service personnel who did not know its age before the cutting.

9. For the Klamath Tribes, Giiwas (Crater Lake) is the home of Llao, god of the underworld. The entire Crater Lake area is a sacred place where members would pray, mourn, hunt, forage, and seek understanding and power. As a child in Kansas, William Gladstone Steel read about Crater Lake and vowed to visit. When he did in 1885, he began lobbying for greater public access to and awareness of the lake. Steel's lobbying led to the designation of Crater Lake National Park as a US National Park. He became superintendent of the park and pushed for greater development to encourage visitors. After three years, he was removed as superintendent.

10. On Saturday, February 27, 1909, Governor George Chamberlain of Oregon resigned from office to be sworn in as a US Senator. By Oregon law, Secretary of State Frank W. Benson was the next in line, however Benson was too ill to immediately assume the role as acting governor. This left Chamberlain's private secretary, Carrie B. Shelton, the next in line. She was, for one weekend, the first woman governor in the US.

11. In 1944 and 1945, the Japanese Imperial Army released over 9,000 long-range balloons carrying bombs or incendiary devices. They were intended to drift through the jet stream to the US Pacific coast. At least 342 reached the US. One killed six people in rural Oregon—the only World War II US combat casualties in the 48 states.

12.   The town of Shevlin, Oregon was owned by the Shevlin-Hixon Company of Bend. It was fully portable. When all timber had been felled in an area, the company loaded the houses on railcars and moved to another logging site.

13.   As I was not able to ask Dr. Hart his preferred pronouns for his youth and his time in medical school, I have tried to honor him as respectfully as possible, knowing that pronouns and identification are incredibly personal and powerful.

14.   During the El Niño event in the winter of 1997-98, sand erosion led to the unearthing of the Neskowin Ghost Forest, remnants of an ancient Sitka spruce forest. The stumps of the Ghost Forest are estimated to be nearly 2,000 years old. Scientists believe that an earthquake or tsunami dropped the land into the tidal zone, destroyed the forest, and preserved the stumps in their original soil beneath the sand. The Thunderbird and Whale is a Tillamook myth that could relate to a large earthquake in that region.

15.   The Mexican mule-pack system was used after the discovery of gold in British Columbia and Idaho during the late 1850s. Walla Walla was a stop for provisions and became a center of mining activity. By 1870, the town had a large population of Mexican mule packers, who were in high demand because of their skills.

16.   At the turn of the 20th century, employment agencies in downtown Spokane charged loggers and miners $1 for a job. This fee was split with employers who would fire the workers after a day or two, forcing the worker to go to another employment agency and pay another fee. This drew the attention of the Industrial Workers of the World (IWW or Wobblies), who established a union hall and quickly began attracting new members. In an effort to thwart the unions, the employment agencies persuaded the Spokane City Council to pass an ordinance banning speaking on the streets, which went into effect on January 1, 1909.

17.   The Fourth Amendment of the United States Constitution: "The right of the people to be secure in their persons, houses, papers, and effects, against unreasonable searches and seizures, shall not be violated, and no Warrants shall issue, but upon probable cause, supported by Oath or affirmation, and particularly describing the place to be searched, and the persons or things to be seized." The American Protective League was

a privately-funded volunteer organization that worked with Federal law enforcement agencies to "stamp out perceived threats to the security of a nation at war." They investigated suspected German sympathizers, as well as the activities of anti-war activists, labor organizations, socialists, and others. At its peak, the APL claimed 250,000 members in 600 cities.

18.   During World War II, Boeing created a fake neighborhood to hide its bomber factory from potential Japanese airstrikes. As the war was coming to a close, Boeing created a photo-op with groups of female employees strolling and picnicking around the ersatz village. *The Seattle Daily Times* dubbed it the "Boeing Wonderland."

19.   The Midnite Mine is an inactive former uranium mine located within the reservation of the Spokane Tribe of Indians. The mine operated from 1955-1965 and from 1968-1981.

Acknowledgments

I would like to thank the amazing team at Cornerstone Press who cared about this project and helped bring it to the world, including Dr. Ross Tangedal, Grace Dahl, Brett Hill, and Julia Kaufman; my poetry group, including Lynne Barnes, Christopher Cook, George Higgins, Kathleen McClung, Vince Montague, Amanda Williamsen, and Maw Shein Win for their great eyes and enduring friendship in prose; Andrew Dugas, Tony Press, and Annie Stenzel for their comments on early drafts; Jerry McCann for letting me write in the stunning home of his uncle Charles Campbell and delve into their family's history, including the writings of their relative Remembrance Campbell; Susan Ito and Leslie Jonath for creating the ideal retreats to burrow into these histories; and my family for teaching me to question and explore.

With special thanks to the following who helped with my research and fact-checking:

Roger Bergmann, Charter Member of the Golden State Gay Rodeo Association, a Rodeo Judge for the International Gay Rodeo Association (IGRA), and a Past President of the IGRA

Adriana Camarena, community organizer and family advocate for the family of Luis Góngora Pat

Perry Chocktoot, Culture and Heritage Director, Klamath Tribal Council

Professor Peter Cole, Department of History, Western Illinois University

Lyra Cressey and **Scott Harding** of the Salmon River Restoration Council

Dr. Harvey Dong, Continuing Lecturer, Asian American and Asian Diaspora Studies, University of California at Berkeley

The family of Luis Góngora Pat

Kate Erickson Green, Associate State Archaeologist, Bay Area District, California State Parks and Recreation

Blaine Harden, author of *A River Lost: The Life and Death of the Columbia*

Stephen Lawton, Hercules Historical Society

Professor Darrell Millner, Portland State University emeritus and former Black Studies Chair

Johanna Ogden, historian and author of "Ghadar, Historical Silences & Notions of Belonging"

Jerelyn Oliveira, State Park Interpreter, Colonel Allensworth State Historic Park

Steven Ptomey, Supervisor, Cultural Resources Program, Great Basin District, California Department of Parks and Recreation

Dylan Vade, co-founder of the Transgender Law Center

Professor Louis Warren, Director, Research Initiative in Environments and Societies, Department of History at UC Davis and author of *God's Red Son: The Ghost Dance Religion and the Making of Modern America*

Gratefully acknowledged are the following publications, where earlier versions of particular poems first appeared:

"After the Gold Rush" first appeared as a San Francisco Public Library Poem of the Day.

"Allensworth," "Six Weeks," and "The People's Champion" first appeared in the Interim *Black Aliveness: Solace & Solidarity* issue.

"Boeing Wonderland" first appeared in the *Gold Man Review*.

"El Honor de Luis" was part of the Wall + Response by the Clarion Alley Mural Project. It appeared online, as part of a film, and in limited edition broadsides.

"Ghost Forest" first appeared in *The Tiger Moth Review*.

"Items Found After Burning Man," "The Meadows," and "Los Mozos Arrieros (The Young Muleteers)" first appeared in *Twelve Mile Review*.

"Miss Atomic Blast" first appeared in *Red Rock Review*.

"Prometheus Felled" first appeared in *South Broadway Ghost Society*, "Language of the Earth" edition.

"Items Found on Angel Island" first appeared in *The Stockholm Review of Literature*.

HEATHER BOURBEAU'S work has appeared in *100 Word Story*, *Alaska Quarterly Review*, *The Kenyon Review*, *Meridian*, and *The Stockholm Review of Literature*. Her work has also been featured in several anthologies, including *America, We Call Your Name: Poems of Resistance and Resilience* and *RESPECT: The Poetry of Detroit Music*. She was a contributing writer to *Not On Our Watch: The Mission to End Genocide in Darfur and Beyond* with Don Cheadle and John Prendergast. She has worked with various UN agencies, including the UN peacekeeping mission in Liberia and UNICEF Somalia. Her most recent collection is *Some Days The Bird*, a poetry conversation with the Irish-Australian poet Anne Casey (2022).

@hfbourbeau

www.ingramcontent.com/pod-product-compliance
Lightning Source LLC
Chambersburg PA
CBHW030511130626
46549CB00007B/2948